# WHO AM I?

# Who am I?

I am graceful and galloping, strong and swift.
I live in a stable.

# WHO AM I?

## By Moira Butterfield
## Illustrated by Wayne Ford

Thameside Press

Distributed in the United States by
Smart Apple Media
1980 Lookout Drive
North Mankato, MN 56003

Printed in Hong Kong

   Library of Congress Cataloging-in-Publication Data
Butterfield, Moira, 1961-
  Horse / by Moira Butterfield.
    p. cm. — (Who am I?)
  Summary: Describes parts of a well-known animal and invites
the reader to identify it.
  ISBN 1-929298-90-0
  1. Horses—Juvenile literature. [1. Horses.] I. Title.

SF302 .B878 2000
636.1—dc21                                      00-024560

9  8  7  6  5  4  3  2  1

Editor: Stephanie Turnbull
Designer: Helen James
Illustrator: Wayne Ford / Wildlife Art Agency
Consultant: Jock Boyd

My hoofs are hard.
My legs are long.
I'm fast and friendly, big and strong.
I gobble apples,
grass and hay.
Then I lift my head and neigh.

Who am I?

# Here is my eye.

I stand in my field and look at the animals nearby. How many sheep can you see?

If I see something that makes me feel scared or angry, I roll my eyes and make my ears lie flat.

# Here are my teeth.

I use them to nibble
plants. I like to eat
the grass in my field.
Sometimes my owner
gives me hay to eat.

I love to munch
sweet foods.
I gobble up apples
and grind them
with my teeth.

# Here are my legs.

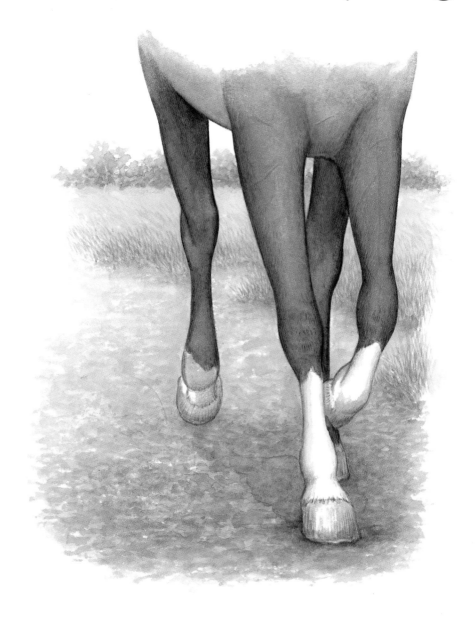

I can walk, trot
or gallop along.
If I am angry, watch
out! I kick hard
with my back legs.

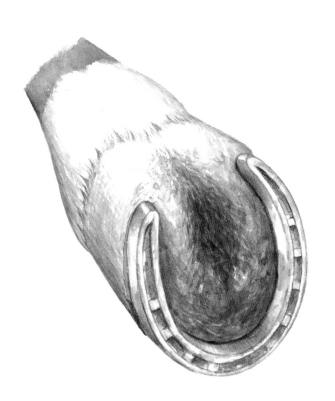

I have four hard
hoofs. Each hoof
has a metal shoe
fitted underneath
to protect it.

# Here is my mane.

It helps to keep
me warm in winter.
If the weather is
bad I stay indoors
in my cosy stable.

In summer I stand
outside in the sun.
I shake my mane
and flick my tail
to get rid of flies.

# Here is my skin.

I am covered in soft, smooth hair. My owner cleans and brushes me. This is called grooming.

I am a red color called chestnut. Not all animals like me are red. What colors can you see?

# Here is my nose.

When I have been galloping I breathe hard through my nostrils. It looks as if steam is coming out of them.

I am good at smelling things. I like to sniff other animals. If you came near I would smell you, too.

# Here is my head.

I have a special way of saying hello.
I stretch out my neck,

open my mouth and...
# neigh!

Have you guessed who I am?

# I am a horse.

Point to my...

long mane

strong legs

large nostrils

pointed ears

swishing tail

hard hoofs

I am a female horse.
I am called a mare.

# Here is my baby.

He is called a foal.
His thin legs are
wobbly at first,
but he soon
learns to stand.

My foal loves to
play in the field.
He rolls, kicks and
runs. I stay close
to him all the time.

# Here is my home.

I live on a farm where there are stables and grassy fields.

Can you see me in the picture?
Look for two foals and three sheep.

# Here are some other kinds of horses.

◄ This is a Shetland Pony. It is very small with a shaggy mane.

► Pinto horses have large markings on their coat, mane and tail.

Some horses are working animals.
Big, strong horses can pull
carts and carry heavy loads.

# Can you answer these questions about me?

What do I like to eat?

How does my owner protect my hoofs?

Where do I live?

What is my baby called?

What happens when I am angry or scared?

What noise do I make?

Can you name some kinds of horses?

How do I get rid of flies in summer?

What do I do when I meet another animal?

# Here are some words to learn about me.

**chestnut** A reddish-brown color.

**gallop** To run fast.

**grooming** Brushing and cleaning a horse to keep it looking neat.

**hay** Dried grass. I like to eat hay because it tastes sweet.

**hoof** My hard foot.

**mane**  The long, shaggy hair that grows along the top of my neck.

**mare**  A female horse over the age of four. A younger female horse is called a filly. Male horses over the age of four are called stallions, and young male horses are colts.

**neigh**  The long, loud sound that I make.

**stable**  My cosy, warm, indoor home.

**trot**  To move faster than walking but slower than running.